THERE IS

ALWAYS

HOPE

A collection of words, thoughts & poems

by

Harper Moon

Cover design: Harper Moon

To all my readers:

First of all, thank you for coming on this journey with me.

I started writing down my feelings and thoughts in 2007, just little things here and there, nothing I ever thought would be of any importance to anyone. As life went on and I faced new obstacles and anxieties, I found myself writing more and more. It was a form of therapy; it calmed me and made my head less anxious and my heart feel less heavy.

I will advise a TRIGGER WARNING: Some poems/thoughts are dark and deep, others are lighter and happy; it was just what I was feeling at that moment in time.

If you are going through a hard time, struggling, I encourage you to speak - to anyone. It doesn't have to be a professional; speak to your friends, your family, just talk. It really helps. Also, write, draw, dance - anything that helps you to express how you are feeling so you don't keep it all inside.

Writing all these poems and thoughts has helped me through my anxiety and depression. And now here I am, sharing my vulnerable moments with all of you in hopes that it may help someone and let all of you know that you are not alone.

Remember, when it seems the light at the end of the tunnel has gone out, it is only because they are changing the bulb to a brighter one! There is always hope! X

SOMEWHERE BETWEEN

Somewhere between life and death
There is a place where
You can right all your wrongs
And fulfil all your regrets
Accomplish all your dreams
Swim the deepest oceans
Climb the tallest mountains
And run marathons back to back.
A place you get to be everyone
You weren´t brave enough to
Become on Earth.

Somewhere between life and death
There is a place
But don´t race to get there
Be patient, it will wait for you.

ALBINO CHILD

Hair of ghostly white
And eyes of crystal clear blue
Your beauty is striking.

Yet you are shy, you are quiet
I can see you trying to
Hide every inch of yourself.

Oh, sweet child,
Own your beauty
Own it with confidence
Turn heads,
Let them admire you.

Fill them with curiosity
And educate them
Stand tall young one
For you are strong
Show them the force you are.

DAYS

Some days I feel like
Everything will be okay
Other days I feel like
I am asking for the impossible.

Days where I can
Take on the world
And days I can´t get out of bed.

Days I can write ten poems
And days I can´t even
Write my own name.

Days where anxiety
Isn´t part of my vocabulary
And days I feel like
It will kill me.

Days I can´t stop laughing
And days where all I want
To do is scream.

But no matter how the day goes
I will fight to see the next one.

OH, CAPTAIN

How many treacherous waters
Must we navigate before we find
Calm horizons again?

How many more storms
Will our boat survive
Before we capsize?

Will we end up drowning
Or will we have enough
Strength to swim
Against the tide?

Oh, Captain, do you think
We will ever see land again?

INKED

A poem inked in black
On a piece of parchment
About a book she once read
Because it changed the way
She saw the world.

A poem inked in blue
On a piece of lined paper
About a beautiful flower
Because the smell reminded her
Of someone she used to know.

A poem inked in green
On a piece of cardboard
About a cloud that resembled an angel
Because she longed for guidance.

A poem inked in red
On a notebook
About how she just wanted to be hugged
Until she felt her worries and anxieties

Melt away leaving nothing but calm
Because everything around her
Seemed so chaotic.

A poem inked in white
On a black piece of paper
Like the colour of her soul
About her feelings
That she tore up as soon as
She finished it
Because it was too much to deal with.

Poems inked on napkins, card,
Notebooks, on the palm of her own hand
And on paper of every colour
That she won´t share with anyone
Because she´s learnt that
Nobody really cares about
How everyone else feels.

WHAT IF

What if the princess didn't need to be saved?
What if she could save herself?
What if she was beautiful,
Strong, kind and clever all at the same time?
What if she was caring but also a warrior?
What if she knew how to defend herself?
What if this was the princess we introduce
Our sons and daughters to
Instead of a princess who
Just waits around to be saved
By some handsome prince?

MOVING ON

Today, I spoke your name
Without chocking up
Today, I read the date
Without my heart racing
Today, I smelt your scent
And my eyes didn´t search for you
Today, I looked through photos of you
And my eyes didn´t turn to waterfalls
Today, I thought I heard your voice
But I didn´t freeze on the spot
I smiled and carried on
Today, I thought I felt your hand
On my shoulder
But my own hand didn´t reach for yours
Because I knew it wouldn´t be there
Today, I looked up to the sky
And whispered I love you
Today, I am starting to move on
But my love for you remains.

WHO ARE YOU WHEN NO ONE IS WATCHING?

When no one is watching
I dance like I did when I was seven
I sing to every song that plays
Even though it´s off key
I skip down the hallway
I still slide down the stairs on my butt
And I run up them like I´m
Being chased by Pennywise.

When no one is watching
I laugh until tears run down my face
I twirl in the kitchen waiting
For the water to boil
And do jumping jacks while waiting
For the microwave to beep

When no one is watching
I watch the same movies and tv shows
I did when I was little because
I find them comforting.

When no one is watching
 I don´t meet any of society´s standards.
When no one is watching
 I am my true self
Wild and free.

LONDON UNDERGROUND

It took me a long time to
Learn how to navigate you
But now I do it with ease.

Each station is different
But the smell is consistent
It´s hard to describe
A combination of damp, various perfumes,
People, fumes and trains
Notice boards everywhere
Filled with quotes and poems
Others with words of warning,
Reminders and eulogies
Ticket machines beep all around
The screech of trains down
The distant passages
Filled with escalators, stairs,
Tunnels and winding passages
 It´s busy and loud
Everybody is always in a rush

Maybe they aren´t that
Different after all
But a creation of pure genius.

LOCKED IN A JAR

Stood on the shelf in a glass jar
Is a tiny girl in a lilac dress
Apple green eyes and hair like fire
Everyone taps on the jar
As they stop to stare
As if expecting her to start doing backflips
Or performing magic tricks

Scared by the constant tapping
And faces being pressed against the glass
She tries to hide herself
With her face pressed against her knees
Hands covering her ears

Waiting for everyone to clear
Before approaching
I can see her tears flowing
I give her a gentle smile as she looks up
On her knees and pressing her tiny hands
Against the glass
"Help me, please help me" she pleaded.

Slipping the jar in to my coat pocket
We quietly escaped

A doll house, her new home,
In my writing room
I put my pen down and watch her twirl
In a sunlit room, her giggles fill the air
Giggles that come with freedom
And happiness.

THE WORLD WE LIVE IN

"You don´t understand the world we live in"
You are quite right,
I don´t understand all the
Racism, homophobia, terrorism,
Violence and abuse that surrounds us.
I don´t understand why innocent
Children die so young
I don´t understand why Cancer
And other illnesses even exist.

But I understand how so many people
End up homeless
Have you seen the price of property?
I understand how so many people
Work themselves to the point of burn out
So many people,
So few jobs.

I understand how the LGBTQ+ community
Still lives in fear,
Do you see the way they are treated?
I understand how so many people
Suffer from mental illness,
Have you seen the standards we
Are expected to meet?

Don´t worry I understand the world.
On some level I understand it better
Than you do.

CHANGE

"You´ve changed"

A phrase that baffles me

Of course I have changed

We all change, like the tide

We live through experiences

We see things

We hear things

And they change us

It is part of life.

Honestly, I would be worried

If I hadn´t changed.

GUILT

Today I felt immense guilt

I almost forgot your birthday

Maybe eleven in Heaven

Is that magical number

Where it stops hurting as much.

Maybe I am finally

Starting to move on.

Or maybe my brain blocked

The date out

Knowing that I still can´t handle it.

PINPOINTING

I was recently asked
When all the anxiety and depression started
Dates flashed through my mind
March 21st 2002,
The day he died of Meningitis,
We were eight and school
Was never fun after that.

Or a few months later
July 23rd 2002
The day I witnessed
My first fatal car crash
I've had anxiety when
I get in to a car ever since.

Or October 15th 2010,
The day you took your life,
Not much made sense after that.

I was seventeen and had
Lost the will to live.
It´s hard to pinpoint exactly
But each date left an
Everlasting impression
A legacy I can´t escape.

POSITIVE THINKING

Everyone told me
"Try not to think about it"
But it was the only thing
I could think about

"Think positive"
That seemed an impossible task
I couldn't see the positive outcome

Then I was told
"Flip any negative thoughts,
Even if it's about something random"
That was the best advice
I have been given in this situation
When negative thoughts brew
I quickly try to think about
Anything else, it isn't always
A positive thought but it

Drags me away from

The depth of despair.

Sometimes even counting is enough.

THAT IS WHERE YOU WILL FIND ME

East of the sun

West of the moon,

That is where you

Will find me

North of the Ocean

South of the sky

That is where you

Will find me

Probably in a daydream

Staring at some distant galaxy

Wishing I was anywhere but here

Or with my nose

Stuck in a book

In some magical world

Or writing a book of my own

Where characters contain

Traces of the person I used to be,

Of the person I wanted to be

And of the person I will never be.

East of the sun

West of the moon

That is where you will find me

Wishing I was anywhere but here.

BE YOUR OWN HERO

I wasn´t myself for weeks
And no one seemed to notice
At that moment I realised
That I needed to learn
To pick myself up
Because no one else
Was going to do it for me.
If I didn´t fight for myself
At three A.M
No one else would
I needed to become my own Hero.

LOST INNOCENCE

When I was twelve

I remember one of my classmates

Telling me

"Once a girl hits puberty

Her body no longer belongs to her,

It belongs to society"

And they were right

Clothes were made tighter

And shorter, more revealing.

The cat calling, wolf whistling,

The remarks, the stares

Totally out of my control

I felt like a piece of art in an exhibition

Where there was nowhere to hide.

I SEE YOU

Sleeping on the street

A small paper cup standing at your feet

They walk past pretending they don't see

Why are they so ignorant?

You don't try to stop them

Your gentle voice goes unheard

But your eyes tell your story

One about every path you've walked

About every tear you have wept

About all the horror you have seen

A cardboard sign to your left

Half hidden out of sight

"I no longer have a wife

Cancer took her life.

I'm an ex Army veteran

I thought my life was all set

I'm not asking for your sympathy

I just want something to eat

It´s tough trying to survive in the city"

How cruel can life be?

You aren´t a criminal

You just lost your way, down on your luck

You greet me with a smile

Which I return and stop to chat for a while.

FAR FROM HOME

When my mother got sick
I found myself over
A thousand miles from home
Suddenly a thousand miles
Seemed so far
And a global pandemic
Making it so much more
Intricate to travel
For months I felt helpless
Until I got to see her again.

CAN WE TURN BACK TIME?

You were in my dream last night

I dreamt you were still here

But after a few minutes

It hit me like a bullet train

You weren´t here

You had still taken your life

And I felt myself start to grieve

For you all over again.

NEWS

I´ve learnt that no news

Doesn´t always mean good news.

Sometimes it means:

Not terrible enough

To have to tell yourself

But

Not good enough

To want to tell you.

ADJUSTING

Today I walked passed your office

Without turning to look for you

Maybe my brain has finally accepted

That you have moved on.

All I know for sure is that

We´ve all found it hard to adapt

But you were right

We WILL be fine.

ARMY OF SHADOWS

Do you ever feel like

You are standing on a roof?

With everything you say,

Everything you do

You step one step closer to the edge

You feel so unsure, so lost

You want to free fall

With the hopes you find

You can fly at the last minute.

What if I told you

These days will pass

That feeling is only an army of shadows

Playing tricks on your mind.

Lead your army of shadows

In to the sunlight and watch them

Slowly shrivel up until they vanish.

Now it´s your turn to shine,

Own your light!

ACCEPTANCE

It took me a long time

To accept and be okay

With who I am

It took me even longer

To say it out loud

Because I knew that

I was letting people down,

That people would be disappointed

But it took me the longest

To realise that my happiness

And mental well being

Outweighed people´s

Opinions of me.

IMPROMPTU CHORUS

You´re not here

By my side

I feel so lost

Without you

You can´t hold

My hands

Through it all.

UNAPPROACHABLE

People don´t understand my personality.
If I don´t join in
They think I am unsociable
Yet if I join in
What I say or bring
To the conversation
Is met with a roll of eyes
Or even annoyance or totally ignored.

I would describe myself as a rain cloud
Capable of producing the brightest rainbow
They describe me as unapproachable,
Maybe I should just resign myself
To bear a sign that reads
"Doesn´t play well with others"

Because each day that passes
I feel more of an outcast.

MOST OF ALL

I want to be perfect

I want to be good

I want to make you proud

But I end up being misunderstood

Never good enough, in your eyes

Never was, never will be

But I don´t mind

I just can´t keep wasting my energy

Trying to become who you want me to be

For I am not her

I am sorry to disappoint

I am my own person

I am strong yet I am weak

I am fierce yet I am tame

I am brave yet I am a coward

I am loud yet I am quiet

I am kind yet I am selfish

I am a superhero yet I am villain

You see, I can never be

Who you want me to be

I just want to be me

But I want you to accept me for who I am

Right now, I don´t know if

Both of those propositions are compatible

But most of all I want to be happy.

STILL HERE

We used to be really close

We used to hang out all the time

But now I see less of you

As you see more of them

But don´t worry

I´ll still be here when you need me.

REPUTATION

I seem to have a reputation

Wherever I go

They´re all different

None fully true

Yet I find myself

Living up to my reputation

Because that is all

People are willing to see me as

And they won´t accept anything else.

DEFEND MY OPINIONS

I can´t keep defending

My views, opinions and hobbies

It is draining

It seems everyone is allowed

An opinion but me

I want to share my views

I want to join in conversations

Without people coming at me

With guns blazing

My defences keep getting weaker

Soon I will give up

I can´t keep defending

The way I see the world.

ANGER

I can feel it rising inside me

Bubbling through my veins

No matter how many

Deep breaths I take or

How many times I count to ten

It never seems to be enough

I can't even tell you why

All I know is that

I am angry…

I wonder if it is

Physically possible for someone

To combust from keeping

All their anger inside.

NOT BELONGING: A CONVERSATION

* I don´t really feel that I belong anywhere

- Look up at the sky,
  What do you see?

* Stars and the moon.

- Did you know that gravity is exactly as strong as it needs to be?

 If gravity were any stronger the universe would collapse on itself

Yet if it were any weaker the universe would be torn apart

Life wouldn´t exist.

What are the odds of that?

* I don´t know…

- About one in hundreds of billion

About the same odds as

You not belonging anywhere.

FRIEND?

You were like every other
Friend I had before you
You wanted to be with me
While it was convenient for you
Until someone better came along
Then you left and didn´t look back
When you left it dawned on me
That we were never friends
Because friends don´t treat
Each other the way you treated me.

SENSORY

My senses are heightened
I can hear the high-pitched
Buzz our refrigerator makes
I can hear emergency vehicles before most
I can see pretty well in the dark
And my eyes pick up on
Everything around me
I can smell burning
Before it reaches the nostrils of others
My sense of taste is pretty sharp
And my hands are sensitive to everything.

But this has its downfalls
Any form of sound is amplified
And too loud
The majority of lights are too bright
Meaning I have a constant headache
Odours leave me feeling nauseous
And my mouth burns with anything

The slightest bit spicy

I freak out if anything wet or sticky

Touches my hands.

I am constantly over stimulated.

When your senses are heightened

The world around you can become

A very overwhelming place.

MY FAVOURITE SOUND

A thunderstorm rumbling in the distance
Echoing along the mountain range
Combined with the gentle patter
Of rain drops against my window
The occasional flash of lightning
Dancing in the sky.

I MISS YOU

There are days when I miss you

I miss our conversations about writing

About astrophysics, about the world

I miss the way we would compare

Opinions on books we had read

I miss the way we would laugh

I miss the way the days felt calm

But then I remember what you did

The anger returns and I no longer miss you.

BE OKAY

I don´t know how to be okay
And I wish I did
Because I hate waking up feeling like this
I wish I could wake up with a smile
And be excited about the day ahead
Yet I awake and count down the hours
Until I can fall asleep again.

MY HONESTY POEM

I was born at the Virgo end of August
That, makes me sensitive,
Hard working and responsible
It also makes me anxious, stressy, critical,
Sceptical and an over thinker.

I have a fear of birds
And failure,
A fear of losing people and
My days are filled with anxiety.

I´m still learning to be okay
With not being good enough
I´m still learning how to
Stand up for myself
I am still learning
It´s okay to make mistakes.

I´m terrible at accepting compliments
I spend my days trying to prove
My right to exist in this world.

I´m clumsy, I trip over my own two feet,
Choke on thin air and drop everything.

I wake up every morning
To dig up my self-worth
But then carelessly bury it
Again throughout the day.

My self- esteem lays in a million pieces
Because I care too much
What other people think of me.

I dread socialising, crowded places,
Loud noises, being out late…
The pressure to fit in is overwhelming

I´m often too guarded
The thought of people
Knowing the real me is terrifying
Because the real me is awkward.

I shove my mistakes and anxieties
In to my closet until
The foundation crumbles
And they all come spilling out
Most of the time I crumble with it
But over time I have become an expert
At rebuilding my life from the rubble.

Hi, my name is Harper,
Most of the time I wish I were invisible
But I am getting better at
Accepting who I am
I still use sarcasm… a lot
And I live my days trying to
Convince myself that I am someone
Worth fighting for.

A LETTER TO MYSELF

I apologise….
I apologise for making you
Put others first when
You own needs weren´t met
For making you help others
When you yourself were falling apart.

I apologise for all the times
I let you just sit there
And take the insults
Without letting you
Stand up for yourself.

I apologise for making you
Join in, smile and laugh
When you were exhausted
And pleading for time alone.

I apologise for not letting you cry
As much or as often as you needed
It´s our strength and our weakness.

I apologise for all the sleepless nights
I made you lie awake while
Your brain played the day´s mistakes
Over and over like a broken record.

I apologise for being so hard on you
For making you feel like
An underachiever
Like nothing you ever did or said
Was good enough
For letting others shatter
Your self-esteem and confidence.

I apologise for making you
Pile on make up
For never telling you that
You look beautiful just the way you are.

But most of all I apologise

For not loving you as much

As I should have

For never telling you

You are not weird

You are unique and unique is good.

Dear me,

I apologise for everything.

I hope one day you can forgive me

For putting us through Hell.

X

DIDN´T MEAN YOU HAD TO

You changed everything,

You messed me around,

Played me like a game,

You broke me

When I asked "Why?"

You simply shrugged

And answered

"Because I could."

I AM

I am a combination of all the words
You didn´t take from my mouth
A combination of all those venomous
Words your tongue spat at me.

I am a combination of everything
You told me not to be
Of everything you told me not to do

I am a combination of all my
Doubts and fears
Of all the daggers you left
Lodged in my back.

I am a combination that makes me
A ticking time bomb.

WHAT I SEE IN THE MIRROR

~~Ugly~~

~~Fat~~

~~Bad skin~~

~~Pointy chin~~

~~Squishy nose~~

~~resting bitch face~~

~~Crocked smile~~

~~Wandering eyes~~

~~Fat thighs~~

Me, I see me.

- Self acceptance

PATHS

If one day you come across my path

And you find that I´ve lost my smile

Come, sit with me for a while

Hold my hand

Come let me know I am not alone

If tears start to fall don´t be too harsh

Have patience for my broken heart

Is still trying to heal

Don´t let me go

Please don´t let me fall

I´m so scared

But if you decide to walk on by

I will understand

I don´t want to drag you here anyway

It´s so dark, so dark

So cold

So lonely

It´s so loud in my head

I can´t concentrate

I can´t think

I need your hand, please don´t let me sink

Everything is on fire I can see it all

I can feel the heat

I can feel the pressure

Please take my hand

Don´t let me go

I´m so scared to fall

Please don´t give up on me.

A NEW DAY

The sun rises bringing new hopes

Opportunities and dreams

It brings new chances to

Smile and laugh

It brings new possibilities

To show everyone how bright you shine.

NUMB

Over the past few days
I have felt nothing at all
Not happy, not sad
Not calm, Not angry
I have been completely neutral
To absolutely everything.

DEAR EARTH

Dear Earth,

I apologise.

I apologise for all the terrible things

We are putting you through

For burning your forests

For melting your ice capsules

For filling your oceans with plastic

For endangering your animals

For hurting your people

I apologise for the way

We are slowly killing you.

WINDS OF CHANGE

We used to be best friends
At one point we were inseparable
And now it´s like we are strangers
We have nothing in common
I miss how close we used to be
Now our words are sharp and blunt
Patience runs low very quickly
I never thought we would end up
Having this type of relationship.

TRACING IT BACK

Everything stems from childhood

The way we talk

The way we act

Our personalities

Our ability to make decisions

From a young age

We all make the decision

To either be like our families

Or to be the complete opposite

All decisions will stem

From those first few years of life.

BATTLES

Our relationship feels like a war

We always seem to butt heads

You no longer understand my life

We seem to have less and less to say

Every encounter is a new battle

And I am getting too tired to keep fighting

I want the war to end

But for it to end we need to cut ties

Yet we both know that won´t happen

But tell me...surly this constant war

Can´t be what you want either.

FALLING IN LOVE

Weeping Willow by Emma Jane Rae

The first poem that spoke to me

The first poem I memorised

From start to finish

From back to front

It opened my eyes to a whole new world

The first poem that

Made me shed a tear

Weeping Willow

The poem that made me

Fall in love with poetry.

QUEEN

Do you have people who

Have inspired you

Even picked you up during your life

Without even meeting them?

For me it was Queen

Freddie, Brian, Roger and John

Their music was always

My biggest comfort

Freddie showed me

That I should be confident

And comfortable with who I am

Brian allowed me to seethat

I could chase more than one dream

Roger taught me to live my life

The way I want to live it

John taught me it´s okay

To lose passion for something

You have to take care of yourself first

Queen comforted me

With the knowledge

That even misfits end up

Fitting somewhere.

THE DEVIL'S HOUR

It's four A.M again

Tears racing down my cheeks

Now I know why they call you the devil's hour

Everything seems so much worse

So much colder

Each thought amplified

Every thought a little bit darker

I just want to sleep

I just want it to stop

To pause for a minute, for a second

I want my head to stop spinning

But nothing seems to stop

No matter how hard I try

Because every night is the same

Every night I fight the demons in my head

The monsters under my bed

How long do I have to fight?

When is is acceptable to stop?

Am I allowed to give up?

Your voice fills my head

"You weren´t raised a quitter

So you better toughen up"

Then tell me

Why is it so hard?

Why is it so dark?

Why is it so confusing?

Shouldn´t it be a walk in the park?

I thought this was meant to be easy

We weren´t born to suffer

I need to get out of this vicious cycle

I need to get my head straight

You drain too much energy from me

But soon the sun will rise again

And I will live to see another day

How many more four A.Ms will we fight?

Will you get me in the end or

Will you give up if I fight long enough?

So many questions

So few answers

Now I know why they call you the

Devil´s hour.

TRUST: A CONVERSATION

Me: He trusted you,
    I trusted you.

Him: I´m sorry.

Me: He... trusted... you.

Him: I have to go now
    But I promise I will fix this.

 Me: You can´t fix broken trust.

MENTAL BREAKDOWN

I had a week where

I cried every evening

I cried until I could no longer see

No longer think

Until my whole body shook

And I was hyperventilating

Then I just sat zoned out

Staring into a dark room

For hours on end

Until I finally fell asleep

The next morning

I would get up and carry on

As if nothing had ever happened.

MORNING MANTRA

I am strong,

I am beautiful

I am clever

I am successful

I am worthy

I am capable

I am enough

Repeat as many times as necessary.

SINKING

I go through the day

With a violin in one hand

A white flag in the other

Trying to stay afloat

On this rocking vessel

But the waves are getting bigger

Throwing me against the rails

I am going under at a rapid rate

Yet I can´t seem to abandon ship

I feel like the last musicians

On the Titanic

I will go down with my ship.

FIXING YOU

I think once I accept

That I can´t fix you

My life will become easier

Lighter, I won´t be carrying that weight

Heavy on my shoulders

But at the moment I can´t seem to let go

Of the guilt I feel

When I think about taking a step back

Nevertheless sooner or later

I am going to have to do

What´s best for me.

OCTOBER

It's the first day

Of the most dreaded month of the year

One filled with so many

Dates and anniversaries

But for all the wrong reasons

I dread you October

You challenge my mental

And emotional strength

And we both know that is where

I fall short

Dear October

Please be kind this year.

Love Harper x

GUILT

Recently I took a mental health day

I let myself stay in bed

To read and sleep

To sleep and read

And even though I knew

This is what I needed to avoid

Burning out and a mental breakdown

I still couldn´t shake that immense

Feeling of guilt that I wasted a whole day.

HEARTBEAT

The beat of my heart

So steady yet so loud

I can hear it pounding in my ears

Proof that I am still alive

Evidence I am surviving another day

Confirmation that I am trying my best

Validation that I am worth every breath I take.

WILL POWER

I have so many dreams
And ambitions
I want to speak Korean fluently
I want to run a marathon
I want to do a triathlon
I want to learn about astrophysics
I want to sell my paintings
I want to travel the world
I want to get a degree
I want to be able to play
Guitar, piano and drums
I want to become a song writer
And I have the capacity to
Accomplish them all
But I lack something important
Will power
I lack the self discipline
To make my dreams become a reality.

SELF BELIEF

Recently I have started

Working on something

I should have developed years ago

Self belief

When I come face to face

With something challenging

I no longer tell myself

That I don´t have a chance

I stare the obstacle straight in the face

And tell myself that

I am capable of overcoming this

From now on I vow

To give every challenge my best shot.

AUTUMN RAIN

The smell of rain fills the air
 Big heavy drops start to fall
 You bring with you
 Strong gusts of wind
 Sending chills through my body
 Blowing leaves off the trees
 Allowing them to float
 In rippling puddles
 Mini lakes of orange and yellows
 Creating much needed calmness.

NONSENSE POEM

Above

Bubbly

Clouds

Destiny

Enlists

Feelings

Great

Happiness

In

Joy

Karma

Leaves

Many

Noticing

Oceans

Parting

Quietly

Radiantly

Spreading

Tranquillity

Under

Various

Waves

Xennials

Yearn

Zen.

PARENTS´ WHITE LIES

Peeing in the pool turns the water purple

Lies turn your tongue black

Eating spinach makes you strong

An apple tree will grow in your tummy

If you swallow the pips

Santa comes down the chimney

Eating the crust gives you curly hair

Don´t forget to eat your carrots

Otherwise you won´t be able to

See in the dark

Now behave, I have eyes in the

Back of my head

The moon is made of cheese

Leave your tooth under the pillow,

The tooth fairy will come

Angels are just bowling,

No need to be scared

Very clever, well played mum and dad
Every child was fooled longer
Than they care to admit.

HAIKU

Wake up each morning

And see the sun rising high

Drops of dew melt away.

I´M SORRY I COULDN´T WALK THEM ALL

Deep in the forest different paths diverge
Each one leading somewhere different
Four routes lay ahead of me
The first covered by thick trees
Creating scary shadows
Shall I take this route or one of the others?

Sun shines on the trail straight ahead
But I shouldn´t let that sway my decision
The road is a steep incline

To my right a winding lane
With every turn a new adventure awaits
I am intrigued

A mysterious mist floats from
The lane to my left
How unusual, how mesmerising

Each one is whispering my name
The path diverges deep in the forest
I´m just sorry I couldn´t walk them all.

LETTER POETRY

Let´s seize the day

Your dreams await

There will be challenges ahead

Don´t let that put you off

For there are many opportunities

Still to grab

Before the curtain falls.

PREVIEW

Where I work there is an old lady

Who comes in quite regularly

She spends hours looking

At every single book

Chatting away to herself

With everyone avoiding her like the plague

I often wonder if she is there

As a preview of how my future will be.

FOR THE BEST

When I left home and moved country
I didn´t do it because I didn´t love my parents
I did it *because* I love them
I knew that if I had stayed where I was
Life would have been very different for them
By moving away I allowed myself
A second chance at life
By moving away my parents
Still have a daughter.

ANYBODY BUT MYSELF

I have days where

I hate being myself

I wish I could be anybody

But me

I sit and try to imagine

What my life

Would have been like

If I had made different choices

Smarter choices

If I had chosen what was right

Instead of what was easy

I cuss myself over and over again

Because my life could have been so different.

RECLUSE

I can´t help thinking

That running away

Cutting ties with everyone I know

Everyone´s life would be a lot easier

Less stressful

I want to become a hermit

A total recluse

Just me, myself and I

I think everyone would be happier.

REMINDER TO SELF

Stop complaining

Stop complaining

Stop complaining

Stop complaining

Stop complaining

Stop complaining

Stop complaining

A) Nobody cares

B) It could be so much worse.

NEUTRAL

I don´t necessarily want to die
But I am not putting as much effort
Into living as I probably should
I can see myself ruining and wrecking
But I can´t seem to stop myself.

FEAR

My fear was that you would leave me

My fear was that you would take

My magic shop with you

My fear was that the confidence

You gave me

Would disappear along with your smile

My fear was that where you made me see

Colour I would only see black and white

My fear was…

My fears came true.

MASKS

Select your mask for the day
Quickly, you don´t want to be late
Happy? Placid? Tranquil? Indifferent?
Which one are you going to choose?
Now, off you go, face the day
Remember to stay in character

Well done,
You made it through the day
You are home, take off your mask
Relax, take a breath
You are safe here
No one to judge you.

DEEP DOWN

"You are not asexual,

You are afraid to fail

That´s your problem"

I was so angry

When you let those words

Slip out your mouth

Angry you won´t accept me

But even angrier that deep down

There is a very small chance

You are right.

ACCEPT US

Everyone thinks they have the right

To tell an Asexual or Aromantic person

That they are only like that

Because they haven´t met

Mr or Mrs Right yet.

Yet I don´t hear them tell

A gay man he is only gay

Because he hasn´t found

Mrs Right yet…

Is it really that hard to accept Asexuality?

DEAR FOUR YEAR OLD ME

Dear little one,

Life is going to be tough

No one will tell you

How people are going to use you

How so many of your dreams get lost

How hard it is going to be

There will be times

When it steals your smile

But never give up,

You will get through this

You are strong

I wish I could protect you

From all the pain and hurt

You are going to face

But I need you to go through this

And come out the other side

To grow and become someone

You can be proud of.

TEACHING IN DISGUISE

I was hoping that people

Would show me exactly

What I wanted from life

Instead I found

That people showed me

Exactly what I didn´t want from life

But now I know exactly who

I want to become.

PROTECT AT ALL COSTS

As your older sister
It terrifies me that
My arms won´t be long enough
To protect you

Your happiness is my happiness
I wish I could take
All your pain and sadness
You will always be little in my mind
Yet, I look up to you
You inspire me to do better
I feel such pride in everything you achieve
In you I have a friend for life

As your older sister
I feel a huge responsibility
And obligation to keep you safe.

CHILDHOOD INNOCENCE

When I was a child I used to believe
That clouds were made of marshmallow
Fluffy ones I could float upon
And glide through the sky

And there was a man who lived on the moon
A man I bid goodnight to each evening
Whose job it was to protect people
As they slept
I believed he had the best job in the world.

WHO ARE YOU?: A CONVERSATION

- Who is she?

+ She is an angel

  Caring and giving

  Generous and loyal

  Talented and hard working

* Her? She is the daughter of Satan

  A demon in her own league

 Selfish, arrogant, dishonest

 Ignorant and lazy

- Tell me dear,

  Who are you?

> See that depends

  On who you ask

  I am an angel to some

  Devil to others.

BOREDOM

Do you ever get bored of living?

Not like wanting to die

But nothing seems exciting any more

Nothing holds your attention for too long

Everything seems so pointless

You just feel constantly tried and drained

Wishing you were a bear

Wanting to hibernate

In the hopes that when you awake

You would have recovered

The joy you once had for life.

WATCH YOUR BACK

Shhhh, stop crying

Don´t let them hear you

Wipe those tears

Calm your breathing

Relax your shoulders

Stop shaking,

Stop shivering

If they find you

They will ask so many questions

Like prying vultures

Waiting to find you

At your most vulnerable

Don´t give them the satisfaction.

SHOWER

I hate showering

Because I am forced

To look at every inch

Of my own body

And I despise it

It reminds me of

My love hate relationship with food

The feeling of guilt

About needing to exercise more

Rushes over me

How an inch or two off my thighs

Would make a big difference

So I stand with my eyes closed tight

Hoping the hot water

Will melt some of it away.

DESSERT

I don´t deserve you,

I haven´t earnt you

I eat you anyway

To avoid awkward questions

But I feel guilty

With every bite I take

I feel disgusting

I loathe myself

The more I eat.

TOMORROW

Tomorrow will be better...
Tomorrow will be better...
Tomorrow will be better…

But what if it´s not
What if it doesn´t get better
What if I am stuck
In a cycle of bad days?

FORGIVENESS

I wish I could forgive you

For the way you make me feel

And always have

For the way you treat me

I wish I could forgive you

But that would mean

Having to forgive myself

For taking so long to do so

And I can´t seem to do that.

THINGS I HAVE BEEN CALLED

Bossy

Whore

Bitch

Unapproachable

Stressy

Annoying

Weird

Arrogant

Lazy

Unappreciative

THINGS I AM

Strong

Independent

Hard working

Tryer

Creative

Good listener

Clever

Kind

Unique

I SEE YOU PT. 2

No sign

No cup

All your worldly possessions

In the rucksack by your side

A ukulele in your hand

A sweet melody captivates me

In an eerie way

As night creeps in

I approach cautiously

Partly because I don´t want

The music to stop

Partly because I know

You want money

But I can´t offer you that.

"I´m sorry, I have no change

But I got you something to eat and drink"

I hear the words leave my mouth

You smile kindly at me

"That is amazing,

 I really appreciate it

 You are the first person

 To stop today

 Thank you so much"

 I carry on walking

 A wave of mixed emotions

 I am full of guilt I didn´t give you more

 I am happy I stopped

 I am angry so many walked past

 Without a glance.

APPRECIATION

I am not a very touchy feely person

Selective about who I hug

Even the ones I love the most

Often fail to make the cut

But I have come to realise

That I show my affection in other ways

Hidden in pictures I create

In handmade treasures

Written in a poem

I now realise

I am not unappreciative

Or unaffectionate

I just express it in a different way.

INSTINCT

"But before he could dwell

On such thoughts

The world before him

Was swept out of sight

And he become lost

In a world of darkness" *

A world much darker than

Any thought he had ever had

He found that he had to trust himself

Battling keep the voice

In his head at bay

Deep down he knew

That as long as he kept moving forward

He would see light once more

There was a fight ahead

But this was not one

He was willing to lose.

* This poem was suggested to me as challenge.
Take the last sentence from a book you have
recently read and use it as the start of a poem.
My first verse is an extract from a wonderful
book called INSTINCT by JAMES CARTER.

LEST WE FORGET

To every man and woman

Who has fought for their country

Has seen, witnessed and lived

Through real horrors of combat

Who struggled to re-adapt

Back in to our fast-paced unforgiving society

I thank you for you service,

Your bravery and dedication

We owe you so much.

WHAT DO YOU WANT TO BE?

Did you ever get fed up

Of being asked

What you want to be when you are older?

What was your answer?

A teacher?

A doctor?

A policeman?

A super hero?

An actor?

An astronaut?

I learnt that the answer

Never really mattered

There was always someone

Who would disapprove.

THE DAYS OF OUR LIVES

Let us live a thousand suns

Let us breathe a trillion breaths

Let us soar through the sky

And swim all the oceans

Let us see all the wonders of the world

Let us hear all of nature´s sounds

Let us live the days of our lives.

TEARS

Tears of sadness

Tears of happiness

Of frustration

Of anger

Of worry

So many emotions

For the same result.

HOME

Born in one country

But raised in another

What if you don´t fit in

Where you were raised

And you no longer belong

Where you were born?

Going back and forth

On a bridge between

The two countries

Not knowing where to call home

What happens if you never find

Where to call home?

What if you end up getting stuck

On the bridge forever?

DECEPTION: A CONVERSATION

* How are you feeling?

- ~~Tried, anxious, worried~~
~~Defeated, useless, drowning~~
~~Overwhelmed, angry, alone~~
~~Not good enough,~~
~~Stressed, Fragile~~
I´m fine

PET PEEVE

The way you love

To constantly prove I am wrong

The sparkle in your eyes

The joy in your voice

The sly smile on your face

You don´t seem to care it upsets me.

.

IT IS WHAT IT IS

"It is what it is"
People who use this phrase
They are strong
They have learnt that they can´t control
Circumstances outside of them,
It no longer affects them.

Like the silence between
Two ticks of a clock
They get on with their lives
Even when everything
Collapses around them
They will just say
It is what it is
And battle on.

DEAR READER

You are fierce

You are strong

You´ve been dragged through Hell

But you´ve clawed your way back

You´ve been torn down

Yet you rebuilt yourself without hesitation

You´re a fighter

You´re a warrior

You never give up

You´re a goddamn superhero

Let the world burn if it makes you happy

Remember don´t let anyone push you around

Be brave and stand up for yourself

Even if it means standing alone

You are worth every breath you take

So stop trying to prove

Your own right to exist in this world

Light up the world with your smile

Show them how brightly you can shine

Show them your full potential

Do what makes you happy

It´s YOUR life!

It´s okay,

I am on your side

Do you trust me?

Here, take my hand

Close your eyes

We´ll make sure only good days survive

Take a deep breath, count to three

You made a mistake but it´s alright

We´ve all made mistakes

Don´t beat yourself up

I´m still by your side

I will always be there cheering you on

Even when everyone else walks away

You´ve got this

I know you are going to be okay

You´re a fighter

You´re a warrior

You never give up

You´re a goddam superhero.

ACKNOWLEDGEMENTS

Firstly, I would like to thank everyone who encouraged me to keep writing after releasing my first book.

Secondly, thanks to Helen for encouraging me to chase my writing dreams, for listening to my worries and woes, and for giving me the confidence to believe in my own abilities. Also, thank you for editing this up for me!

And, finally, thanks to you for joining me on this journey!

X

Printed in Great Britain
by Amazon

74523182R00081